C000056104

ALCESTIS
in the
UNDER
WORLD

Also by Nina Murray

Minimize Considered

ALCESTIS
in the
UNDER
WORLD

NINA
MURRAY
POEMS

CIRCLING RIVERS
RICHMOND, VIRGINIA

Copyright © 2018 by Nina Murray

All rights reserved. No part of this book may be reproduced in any form, including electronic, without permission in writing from the author.

CIRCLING RIVERS

PO Box 8291
Richmond, VA 23226
CirclingRivers.com

ISBN: 978-1-939530-12-7 (hardcover)
Library of Congress Control Number: 2020937873
ISBN: 978-1-939530-07-3 (paper)

Cover and inside map of Moscow, copyright © 1963 by Richard Saul Wurman. From *The City, Form and Intent: being a collection of the plans of fifty significant towns and cities all to the scale of 1:14400*. Raleigh, NC: School of Design, North Carolina State University, 1963 via David Rumsey Historical Map Collection | davidrumsey.com

The following poems were first published in...
"Moscow metro" in *The Harpoon Review*
"memory theater" in *Mulberry Fork Review*
"for L.B." in *Figroot Press*
"Leon Bakst" in *Ekphrasis*
"Silva Rerum" XIII and XIV in English and Lithuanian translation
    10. *Druskininkai Poetic Fall Festival Anthology 2012*
"trust not the dawns" in *Poetry Blue River*
"sometimes I dream of my father's garden"
    in *Totopos Poetry International*
"Alcestis discovers her colonial consciousness"
    in *Adanna Literary Journal*

Visit CirclingRivers.com to subscribe to news of our authors and books, including book giveaways. We never share or sell our list.

Contents

TWO

THREE

ALCESTIS
in the
UNDER
WORLD

memory theater

I. orthodoxy

A collage made with postcard images of Ronald Reagan—Reagan smiling
under the brim of a white cowboy hat, Reagan leaning against a saddle
slung over a weathered three-rail fence, Reagan gazing into the distance
in the light of a campfire—overlaid on a half-finished paint-by-numbers
picture of black-eyed Susans.

II. domesticity

A set of unused thank-you cards, printed with the fretwork patterns
from the 1754 edition of Thomas Chippendale's *The Gentleman and
Cabinetmaker's Director* owned in the colonies by Edmund Dickinson of
Williamsburg. Dickinson died in the Battle of Monmouth. Each of the
four cards, presumably in anticipation of a personal message, has been
stamped with an image of a honey bee in place of the signature.

III. divination

An archival box of brown cardboard which contains five quarter-inch
labradorite beads, a 1920s manual of kennel management, a worn bouquet
of thistles spray-painted silver, and a single owl feather. The feather
belongs to *Athene cunicularia*, a burrowing owl.

IV. competence

A performance by a fit man, wearing only hunter-green-and-navy plaid
cotton boxer shorts. The man uses a large kitchen knife to cut in half a
white oval pill—Ambien—carefully, so as not to shatter it. He is back-lit
by a Cavaliers–Celtics game on TV. LeBron James has 37 points with over
two minutes remaining.

V. verdure

An abstract hand-embroidered tapestry in gobelin stitch which evokes
the deciduous forests of central Maine. The glimpses of blank base canvas
engender the same delight as discovering a mushroom, tossed off the back
porch into the blueberry thickets last night, gone this morning.

VI. conveyance

A tonal variation in F-major which reflects the pattern of light and shadow
as observed by a passenger traveling south on Everett Pike at 8:07 am
in July. A whiff of marijuana smoke registers at some point although no
observable source of it can be found except a sign on the shoulder that reads
"Mowing." The doctor on the radio says caffeine is the second-most traded
substance in the world.

ONE

All the others are only her narrow path
down which she comes, and comes—(soon she'll be
there in his arms, that have opened in pain)

But as he waits, she speaks: not to him.
She speaks to the god, and the god listens...

— Rainer Maria Rilke, "Alcestis," translated by A.S. Kline

memory theater

VII. Alcestis at the feast

Tsaritsyno is a palace and park in south Moscow,
founded in 1776 by order of Catherine the Great.

the first truly warm weekend of the year
the air   the sun and the effervescent lindens all tolerant
of the picnic we spread among them
but the breeze enough to drive the water's surface
in marching cohorts against the efforts of boaters

the men—prematurely out of shape—at oars must
exert more than would be consistent with the anticipated
Edwardian nature of this leisure pursued
for their children draped over the prows
lured by the swirl
of chill water
almost within the reach of outstretched fingers
and the women who brood
over their clandestine
discontent obscured by the delicate act of say
peeling an egg

the promenade resplendent in lipstick-gloss tulips
the fountain's projections timed to the last
generation's beloved French pop tunes
the imperial palace itself a crown of fresh masonry
upon the hill: the Empress having never set foot
in the rooms   their opulence guessed-at
by the construction crews who left undisturbed
the hooks driven into the walls

by the dwellers of a commune decades ago
to string laundry lines

on the other shore
a crowd impugns
the task of a keeper
who's brought the fowl from their winter roosts
mallards garganeys and coots
spread away on the water   a trail of wayward crumbs
he carries each bird down a short muddy slope
in outstretched arms hands clasped
over the wings—his grip reassuring
when he handles a few yearling swans
attenuated in their tarnished plumage
like antique coffee-pots—
and then a fully grown bird
—he slips
the swan flaps once
twice
the wings beat off the hands
and he's on the ground

the bird unfolds
a white-hot hissing brand of the wild
it aims itself at the thin hide of illusion
dismissive of man   plans and rules
snaps at the keeper's heels
surveys the alien masses
turns
and commands the water

surveillance detection reports

1

I took a cab to meet the Professor at a downtown coffee-house,
where he was already waiting, having ridden his scooter
and ordered cake, with raspberry reduction on top, for us to share.
I wanted to learn about healthcare financing, but we talked about bears
     instead—
the Professor's brother lives in Kamchatka and likes them. Two men took
the table behind the Professor's back where I could see them. The older,
round-headed and portly, placed his cell phone on the table, microphone
pointed at me. The younger was fit in a way that suggested carrying buckets
of concrete and doing chin-ups the army way. I felt compelled to rule
out the chance they were lovers—and did, when I caught a glimpse
of the young man's hands, his neglected cuticles, bitten nails. The men
ordered sandwiches and conversed, no papers in front of them, no shared
     laptop.
I told the Professor his brother made me think of Jim Harrison—
a mensch, in love with bears and the woods. The Professor asked
if the pink cotton sweater he wore made him look gay. I said it did not.

2

The women on the cruise with us could have been mother and daughter
but they didn't bicker. Only one had a purse.
The other kept her hands fisted in the pockets of her olive coat.
They didn't speak to each other. Our friends talked
about state tax rates, retiring to Idaho, vacation plans. The Kremlin
floated into view portside. The women, starboard,
kept their eyes fixed on the unspooling ribbon of the granite embankment,
impervious to my imagination that wanted
intensely to give them a better reason to be there.

Our cruise boat paused under a bridge to let through a barge,
low and loaded high with scrap-metal and dirt. We talked
of corruption in the construction sector and the coming flu.
When the boat docked, I missed the moment when the women left.

    3

I've been shown surveillance footage from an unlit room:
grayscale, bodies in feathered outlines like ghosts. I think
I know where the camera is in the bedroom, its view a pit
where we wander at night like souls in Elysian fields, entitled to oblivion.
I tell myself to become an empty contour, a skin—
let the lens have my back, your fingers,
the cursive of ribcage, stomach, hip.

And the one who watches—does he know
what it takes to be in his gaze (in my mind, it is
always a he), to erase enough not to care what's
being seen?

I wonder also if a second woman exists,
my body double, with eyes that watch
the watcher, judge his hard-on, the spit
he swallows, if she laughs, or teases,
or leaves.

Moscow metro

the Shakespeare scholar says
we are no longer an audience
but a crowd of spectators
—especially here, I think,
facing each other on a subway car
each buffeted by his own thunderstorm
on the seat's meager moor
and all
in mute contract not to pry
not to hear the lines
we can see each other mouthing
a string of spectacular specters
only the man in the corner corporeal
head bent over a large bruise-edged
bouquet of white asters
small petals tangled like hair

the Sapsan express

I think:
the railyard covered with snow and vacant
is a page in an exercise book
the inky raised lines tempting the hand
into intersecting traps

I think:
the peaked gray roofs
of small houses under this lilac sky
are triangular tracks of giant
iron-clawed birds
that spooked and flew up
rending the cloth of the hill

metaphors to fill time on the train
in the speeding cocoon
of suspended purpose

a blur: a feather twirls
in the locomotive's wake

St. Petersburg

October, 2016

The Admiralty's spire
the gilded needle
of the imperial compass

pea-gravel under foot in Alexander's Garden
dutifully refracts erratic sunlight onto
the shabby gentility of urns
the fountain's elegant arcs list in the wind

I contemplate a different life
one attained through accomplishments
more after my own heart
one whose landmarks are more recognizable

but in which still
there's you
and boxwoods
and the small crunch of gravel

things on leashes

her pink umbrella
has a tether just as pink
she lets the frilly thing
roll down the sidewalk
cartwheel in the wind
a timid wobbly sail
she waits for it to tug
then reels it in

she's waiting for the bus with me
she's seven, maybe six
as utterly composed
well-groomed and rigged
as a small frigate

the breeze
taunts traffic
the umbrella bobs
we contemplate
the things we cannot have
hers is a dog, I think

memory theater

VIII. vexillology: variation on a theme by Mark Strand

the pennants hoisted by maples to announce their arrival into the fall

the flickering signal of the setter's tail that charts the shorn field

the resolute chevron of the entrenched pocket silk, the bulwark of style

the St. George's ribbon in flimsy fesses on commuters' backpacks and
    rearview mirrors
marooned like the vacuous bubbles of shed beetle shells

the banner on the metro wall in coagulated drops of scarlet mosaic: Lenin's
    bellicose ghost

the stiff sheet of the paper's front page pieced from fragments like soldiers'
    quilts stitched from clean bits of despoiled uniforms

the pinstripe buntings of our umbrellas set out to dry side by side

the heavy curtain we draw in surrender as we turn ourselves blind
    to the coming winter

a mediated christmas

1

light comes in
smooth as a cat
worries the tinsel
        bats at the gift wrap
fits itself into the cracked shells
of last night's intimacies

it'll be here—dallying—
when we rise to the new day

2

we carry on: the cards, the calls,
roast and cocktails, sticky scone dough—
tap a heart on each hatted and antlered dog—
one eye on the timer, one on The Times,
which alerts: reading fake news, Pakistan
tweeted a nuclear threat. and the oven's warm.

memory theater

IX. Alcestis discovers the hierarchy of Soviet republics

I am five and ethnically ambiguous: dark eyes,
wide cheekbones, but indisputably Ukrainian and thus
not classifiable as Gypsy, or Asiatic. Also,
exceedingly dutiful, so I don't mind when it's decided
I am the best fit for the role of the Uzbek girl in the pageant
for the International Day of the Solidarity
of the Working Class. But the model in the picture book
wears at least two dozen braids and harvests cotton, whereas
my hair often gets me mistaken for a boy and I've never laid eyes
on a crop. I am an architect's child in a city full of decrepit baroque
cathedrals.
          My costume's embroidered cap, comes with
shoe-laces sewn into the rim and braided down, so problem solved.
I'm delighted—exactly until I see the girl in the Russian
costume: she's blonde, and has down-trimmed
satin sleeves, a splendid crown like a flattened onion dome,
in glitter and gold.
The cotton-picking dance shows
the important contribution of the Uzbek people to the GDP.
I turn my hands to showcase tufts of cotton wool
and become alert to the irony. The Uzbek girl and I—
just two subalterns, interchangeable and for the moment, swapped.

collection needs

between the church
and the West-facing Lenin
I carry
rabbit legs to be stewed into dinner
slow-gaited through the shirtless swarm
—skateboarders
helmetless males
in scuzzy sneakers
I size up their torsos:
pale
whiplashed as they ride
erratic arcs
on granite
       sway
a colony of sea anemones
I calculate
life expectancy at their likely age
assess combat readiness
failed flips
miss me—but only just

tomorrow
I will walk the other way
as the city's crews
comb the lawns
for depleted juice boxes
cigarettes
broken wheels
mop Lenin's pedestal
edges ground down
chipped where the boards
slipped

all the cards say the same thing

after Greg Kuzma

i open one and it says
i feel lonely and for reasons i don't understand
it feels less lonely to write this card and send it to you
even though i can't remember where you live
and if you take the bus to work in the morning

i open one and it says
for reasons i don't understand it feels meritorious
to keep in touch as if touch were a dark room where we held
hands dancing

i open another one and it says
we have all become a year older
and there's been so little for which we can take credit
our children have gone on existing like electricity
regardless of our knowledge or understanding of them
they roll in the snow outside like pumpkins

our maladies too disregard our need for warning
evolve overnight into conditions and demand
urgent procedures while we wonder
how does that old apple tree feel when a limb breaks under
the weight of sudden ice when its flesh shivers in the open crack
and twists in ways unknown before
unburdened

i open another one and it says i'm sorry
i'm sorry i accorded your troubles the privilege of coming and going
unchallenged i let your calamities nest in my mind

like homeless people in a public library i've been
a spectator i got distracted i failed

i open the last one and it says
may the grace of the season be with you
we love you

trust not the dawns

Now guard the beaches
watch the north, trust not the dawns.
> — Robinson Jeffers, "So Many Blood-Lakes"

a four a.m. run to the airport
I must be the driver's first fare
so he begins to recite the company's greeting
softly in the dark orb of the car
wishing me a good morning
a happy belated unity day
resilient health   fulfilment in personal life
and to all of us he says
a peaceful blue sky above our heads

which is when I resolve not to tip him
for this blithe cold-war formula
his mindless rehearsal of threat
while it is I who must recall
an early spring night in a country that borders his
when I lay listening for the dive of invisible jets
the distant rumble of rocket launchers
shivering because I knew
how open it was—the window of opportunity
deterrence the sound of me swallowing hard
and the steady drift of rain on my window

same to you is what I actually said
he signaled diligently before changing lanes

memory theater

X. Alcestis reviews George Washington's Rules of Civility

Walk not when others stop
leave not behind that which you had accompanied thus far
yet
take not upon yourself
a burden given up upon
by many else.

Spit not in the Fire
as fire will return your spit as hiss
and take offense
more certainly than not

Sleep not when others Speak
sleep not when others—that may be also wise
others when they sleep
won't speak
and neither should you
feel compelled to do so
when sleeping, listen not to others
those voices

Shift not yourself in the Sight of others
nor Gnaw the nails
Shake not the head
rowl not the eyes
wry not the mouth
others will speak when you're asleep

oh yes they will
the others

Run not

Speak not of Melancholy Things
as Death and Wounds,
and if the others
Mention them
Change
if you can
the Discourse

tell not your Dreams
tell someone else's dreams instead
choose dreams
of which you know little,
naught, in fact, and thus can make them up
your own dreams, you cannot tell a single thing
they know better

Speak not in an unknown Tongue
when others speak, do hold your peace
and let them be
the dreams
the others
speaking

Lviv, January 2017

the oracle speaks
through the mouths of blind fish
bivouacked in the subterranean groves
of petrified cedar
that scaffold this city
here unlearned memory's murky
like the call of blood
but the oracle says, not knowing
is the path to perdition

look up:
the sky traps auguries
in the palimpsest of spires

TWO

Yet also there encumbered sleepers groaned,
Too fast in thought or death to be bestirred.
Then, as I probed them, one sprang up, and stared
With piteous recognition in fixed eyes,
Lifting distressful hands, as if to bless.

— Wilfred Owen, "Strange Meeting"

Alcestis in the underworld

what we remember is what we believe
they don't believe in things that we remember
they do remember things we don't believe
and we can speak the things they don't remember

for L. B.

*After the Soviet annexation of the Baltics, the
Lithuanian Embassy to the Holy See persisted and
issued passports over the decades that enabled many to
escape to the West.*

the staff unmoored
the mission overnight a refugee
a rogue

the cable traffic thready as a pulse
it stops
resumes

decrepitude becomes the foe
indoors the oak banisters are buffed
to civic sheen
but ivy infiltrates the garden urns
they ration paper—watermark and cardstock
the Consul vigilant against the first
intimations of arthritis
his cursive as yet unimpeachable
goes on
the dotted lines

the passports claim a nation
stake by stake
this one claims you—your turtleneck, your mullet—
a body

for a country mapped by ghosts

4'33" by John Cage

*4' 33" consist of the sounds of the environment that the
listeners hear while it is performed.*

the fridge—an oscillating hum
the erroneous piano being practiced   upstairs

footfalls   no, rain   in measured succession on the windowsill

receding
exhalations

the final adjustment of the last ice-cube
dropped into the kitchen sink after the dinner dishes
as it cracks and falls into the maw
of the garbage disposal

a lock turns in a door
on the same floor

beyond what I can hear
the rasp of silverfish that undulate across the bathroom floor
the snap of worn-down tweed inside a moth's small jaws

memory theater

XI. sometimes I dream of my father's garden

he never had a garden—still
I dream of him—linen trousers, unsocked feet—
with shears

and coals on the grill
intent on their complicated game of wink
and signal with the wind—

a stripe, a line, a streamer,
a cinder fringe now bristled—
and then gone

the coals I know to be true
the rest—the bees in thrall
to cherry bloom, the dapple
of the sun on his smooth hands,
the man—are dream

St. Nina's parables

With a vision and a cross made of grapevine, St. Nina brought Christianity to the ancient Georgian kingdom of Kartli in 320.

the parable of the fox

for generations they erected towers
for homes
stalagmites of effort
grown like an orchard slowly
year by year
each room smaller than the one below
until I must make of myself a child
a smaller form to feel at home on top

raised so far
I missed the grassy breath
of earth
until the day the glacier shed
an avalanche
worn skin of snow of rocks
the mountain's spine aquiver
and below
our homes like tutting fingers
or imploring hands

I watched through narrow windows
snow lay itself to rest
no view of mountain face
the terrible descent—sliced into eyefuls

at night a fox appeared
sprung suddenly full-armed and sage
from a pagan god's cracked forehead
disoriented
she stared until she must have caught a whiff
of pantry from below
and vanished

only
the breath we both held in
bore the weight of walls
and roof
I learned
my room could hold another

the parable of the hunter

what could possibly be learned from the tale
of how I met a hunter on the road?
of hunters, you know enough—
they are in the snow
knapsacks rolled onto their backs and the town below
they commune with dogs
of me so much less is known

the hunter gave me his coat
—or was it a crust of bread?
a thing hollowed out by what had been there before
patterned with tracks   a trap
for dry basil leaves

clipped nails
sweat
seeds
how did he know
what to give?

when he descends the hills
he carries such different things:
he knows where a rabbit would make a gift
when a seed might sprout a cure
a wolf pup love a man

I am not a hunter
what I carry is always the same
words
only words and more words
I have words for things that are seen—
such words have no need to be heard
and the ones for what is unseen—

mine mean little to others

letters

Ukrainians from Galichyna and Bukovyna came to the U.S. in large numbers in the last quarter of the nineteenth century. Many settled in Chicago.

revelation

I crossed the ocean on the ship of fools.
A White Guard corporal with two gray trotters
shared the hold with a tired Jew,
pharmacist and muralist from Drohobych.
The old man hid his gnarled bluish toes—
he had buried his shoes in the mud of his basement.
In the eyes of his god, lifting his soles
meant giving up rights to return as a master.
I fashioned him slippers of scarves and rags,
and he shuffled off onto Ellis Island.
My own boots, they broke cold sweat
in the frigid fog of idle lines.

I wish I had left more things behind.
And now the herds are leaving the mountains.
The wolves kill watchdogs every night,
and pigeons roost on the church's rafters.

mending

A dead man's coat, this needle in my fingers
a sharpened minus pricking at my nails.
I am but a sum of irreconcilables,
an irksome pile of angles and shadows.

Threadbare cuffs stretched, loops splayed
thin and wide like cheap chops,
splintered bones, greasy buds.
What am I mending?
Particles of skin,
dried sweat, laborious turns of arthritic wrists?
The man was old, he died alone, we shared
his belongings after we patched a funeral
together—a sharp-jawed Irish priest,
Greek grocer for grave-digger, a Cuban cook,
and I, Ukrainian cobbler, a stumbling mourner
with a mouthful of psalms.
I took this jacket.   Made in Buffalo, NY,
and issued by the U.S. Navy. Worn
around the collar, lining pressed so hard
against the seams it blistered, burst.
He must have often clutched the collar tight
against the wind, a man of no illusions,
no rough-throated charms for an abandoned lover.
I do my woman's jobs. I need a wife.

donation

The ancients took great care in crafting executions:
millstones round the neck an extra offense to the pagan spirits
of running water, grinding silently in the brown dust of reed and sedge.
It's only the saint that came up—and what
of the miller?

Then cauldrons of pitch, fat, oil, boiling lead until angels
put an end to the travesty, delivered the martyr frolicking, unscathed.

Were they psalms that St. Hugh sang dripping,
shiny, naked?

Finally, the poisoned blood of his stubborn beloved—
the woman he'd seen beating her linens on the river stones
and who was bled to death from Christ-like wounds.
The irony, the cosmic taunt, the ancients knew
their bare-assed defiance.

After St. Hugh's death, friends shared his bones
which were made into the tools for making shoes.
It was then said about saints the secret art of their sanctification was
the way they studied to subdue their passions and die themselves, an act
    of pure intention.

And now, what is left? A thousand midget deaths
between St. Michael's Day snowstorms
and gaslit alleys, kitchens, Irish cops, Greeks,
groceries, and soot that drops in flakes
each time the northbound train derails the night.

I learn the games, the ball, the base, the cleats—
I put horsehair in left soles for better spring—
can't hear a single bell ring except the streetcar's.

Here, brother cobbler, foreign saint, you were
a convict once—this land has sentenced me a million
times. You left your bones, I give away my shoes.

a boy flanked by hounds

a photograph by John Johnson (b. 1879)

He hasn't yet learned that a pyramid is a body of hopeless
    stability:
although years can nibble and claw at its sloping sides,
they'll just roll off the hounds' smooth haunches. He is
    immutable,

immune, minute, a buttoned-up knot of wires.
The dogs at his sides a matching pair of anchors
and his body they tether a mast, an axis, a spire.

He hasn't yet learned geometry's verdicts and ploys.
He is only a boy flanked by a pair of hounds.
But you, can't you see: the lens is the eye of a Cyclops

come to make him a totem,
a marker to top another bone-filled mound.

at Zima Junction, 1943

The taiga speaks in small voices:
the snapping of tree-limbs trapped in ice
as we fell them, the chip and chime
of fir. My own breath, the caesura between
the ache of expanding my lungs and the fear
of contracting. Mouth, nose, the whole face
wrapped, eyes sun-bleached, this muteness
is also a kind of blindness.
Only the taiga speaks.

A storm—and the trees lie uprooted, naked.
Women
walk among them as if on a battlefield:
we had expected a different kind of death
for these and now
we don't recognize them.

In a hollow left by the roots
we discover a pony—brown and white piebald,
long fur spiked with mud and ice,
grass in his teeth. Anna Ivanovna kneels
close to his nostrils, writes
with her gloved finger in the snow,
ten thousand years.
She cares to remember those things.

At the station father says,
it is amazing how long meat could keep
in the ground here. We wait for
the rations and watch trains pull away
the trees, chains chilled quick into bark.

ash wednesday

in my dream
the Messiah has been reimagined
onto the frescoed fields of streaking blue and gold
late summer sunlight chastened
by the whiff of mustard gas
the battlefield behind him now vacant
he is clean-shaven
hair—trim
minute sharp licks of it distinct on sunburnt temples
the sleeves of khaki uniform rolled up
on his farm boy's forearms
one in a sling
the free hand clasps
a blood-edged book of psalms

He is a man recovered

memory theater

XII. Alcestis at the country house

Summer, *by Nikolai Bogdanov-Belsky, 1911, oil on canvas*

in the distance: the scab-colored ruts of a dirt road
part the unshorn abundance of hay fields,
woods loom—a dark cross-beam on the horizon

middle-distance: the fields resolve into an effort at a lawn,
a Venus, whitewashed each spring, no doubt, by an uncomprehending
village girl until the finely sculpted folds of skin
grow irresolute under the layers of lye, reflects the sun

it is high summer, noon, so the double-braided
daughter of the house must strain against the glare as she draws.
Indoors the dressing table a tableau
of misplaced aspiration: good taste spent
in the cornflowers that cascade off a white-laced bureau,
the mother—goddess—gone

the gauzy ribbon of her hat glows in the darkened room
a lamp, left on in faith

Leon Bakst (born Leyb-Khaim Rosenberg)

the sketch of a harlequin patterned in gold and chartreuse the figure
in suspended animation
a somnolent puppet

bottom right corner blotted
blue paper warped with hardened gouache
ghost of the invisible hand that knocked over the vial
the unheard conversation
perhaps a brush of garment
the patches in the harlequin's costume now in menacing kinship
with the opaque maw below his feet

and then Bakst himself blonde and blue-eyed
bloused and bewhiskered
a *mensch* a prodigal Habsburg
banned from St. Petersburg for the stain of his blood—
the fractured syllables of it
the threads in the diamond lattice of the brilliant costume
the unignorable pool

the ghosts of spies

1. Sidney Reilly

*Born Sigmund Rosenblum in Odessa, is alleged
to have spied for at least four powers. Arrested
and executed by the Bolsheviks in 1925.*

this one stole the fissile
scapula

see him up there back in harness
brush bonemeal like goldleaf
onto the onion dome

a wife and a mistress
on one rope—
hanging out laundry
flat-chested chemises
pantaloons
menstrual rags

the women laugh
mouths full
of forked wooden pegs

2. Mata Hari

Margaretha Geertruida MacLeod, a Dutch exotic
dancer and courtesan. Convicted of being a spy for
Germany, executed by firing squad in France.

look at her
who had worn an asp as a headdress
and eluded corsets—
now lizards lace up
her bullet-holed ribs
iridescent at each
vespertine pirouette

3. Richard Zorge

Working undercover in Tokyo, delivered the
intelligence of the German invasion plans to Stalin
who ridiculed it.

his head in Cassandra's lap,
she delights in prophecies
about the weather
and the affairs of hedgehogs;
he dispatches in code
haiku on the cloistered
contentment of owls

Alcestis in the corpse pose

Always the worst: the instant she must
contract her muscles again, engage the knuckle flexors
that lift her fingers like small boats riding out a swell,
regain the sense of air, restore
proprioception—useful but an imposition
nonetheless, her mind so much more comfortable
in its exile where it rests, withholding judgement,
thinking of Montaigne. She aches,
and wishes for a different corporeality:
an owl, or a fox,
a perfectly evolved kingfisher,
or an otter—a body that would fit
a small, quick hunter's mind.

THREE

And after the commanded journey, what?
Nothing magnificent, nothing unknown.
A gazing out from far away, alone.

— Seamus Heaney, "Squarings: I. Lightenings"

reduced circumstances

1

the snow-trimmed peacocks on the zoo's gate
are the day's only available metaphor:
elaborately cast,
engraved and chased,
exulted kin to rutting
open-mouthed elk
paraded in the bas-relief below them
reverberant with days
on which the wings   the tails
felt made of lighter stuff—
bone
sinew
feather

2

it's been banished:
the chatty tribe
of loose-haired valkyries in my head
astride irreverent
swift-footed mares

mind now hollow
a great cathedral
where dusk pools
around the imposts
vacant confessional booths
throb
with remembered

hoofbeats
and god
holds his breath

3

the meager offerings
of capillary blood
small red worms
sluiced out
onto a tissue every morning
are limpid
lifelike simulacra
of something sacrificed
and not enough

Alcestis returns

The door whence the son left home, confident and puff'd up;
The door he enter'd again from a long and scandalous absence,
diseas'd, broken down, without innocence, without means.
— Walt Whitman, "Song of the Broad Axe"

the shape that I vacated
held still—a doorway
while I went through
and then returned a different figure
one that no longer fit
into what had been so solidly framed out
—but no one
raised the roof beam

so now here I am:
an object
an objection
and a jest
a woman in a taxidermied hide
that must be donned to soothe the skittish

I dream what this pelt dreams:
to be its own thing
a wolf   an antelope   an otter
a quick ghost fox who laps, for the first time,
the ghost snow sparkling on the Stygian water
and stops to marvel

I must not be seen if I'm to be
still recognizable

flights

1

over the heads of very tall men—
a basketball team shuffle-footing it through
the boarding line to Tallinn—
a pigeon takes off
with a vaguely hydraulic whirr,
a contented bird
with no intention to leave

2

piebald fields
race by
in streaks of blue
tan
snow dreaming of being water again
in the rippling shadows
the land is taut
where boulders bulge
like the knuckles of a restless god
the sky ennobling
and chaste—
an arctic

inventory: labeled boxes

#1. Books. Half a dozen pens—
all missing from other locations
where once they were expected to be found.

#2. Magnets. Index cards, so called
because they point to phenomena beyond themselves
but still in the realm of the tangible,
charting the call-signs of our shared imagination:
contrition
>>> tether

>>> clairvoyance

#3. Christmas lights. Whisk.
Two pigeon eggs, ossified.

#4. The chair that had been in the corner
and then in the only spot in the apartment from which
the lake could be seen
and had held many hours of reading, firmly
and with assurance,
all despite a broken leg.

#5. Yarn. Yardstick. Mascara.

#6. Hooks. Screwdriver. Lace.

#7. An object consisting of pine cones,
rocks, and hazelnuts, some of them cracked
and spray-painted dull gold.

#8. Books. Bread knife. Pendulum.

#9. A dog leash. I learned from my father
to be a material dreamer. Buy the buttons,
he used to say, for the coat you want to have made.
I had a dog already. And yet I keep dreaming.

#10. Wind chimes. Ashtray. Wasp.

how to fail at gardening

first, remember: the garden knows so much more than it lets on

I have watched mine bloom for my mother
and respond to my own ministrations
with indifference that's nothing short of imperious

the garden has no time for your delusions
it most certainly reserves the right to determine
what withers and what grows
the amount of cultivation you invest
is of no concern
to the garden

do contemplate the quiet stoicism of weeds
nothing blooms that's not ironic
the garden is a million opportunities for you to be wrong

it is quite possible that you are the distraction
from the garden's work

the garden suffers from acedia, perhaps, and you
are its obsessive thought
its noontime demon out to tease

inveigle and tempt
inspire it to hate its circumstances

isn't it likely that
the garden wonders
what it would take to have you gone
for good?

memory theater / silva rerum

*(Lat. "the forest of things"—a multi-generational
chronicle, kept by many Polish noble families from
the sixteenth through eighteenth centuries)*

XIII. dogs

Five mysteries hold the keys to the unseen...
— Salman Rushdie

Five breeds of dogs are kept in our lands
The fast hound who can see far and flies in pursuit
of a flickering fox
the hunter of vision.

The bloodhound that persists on a trail
never falters
the steadfast courser.

The exuberant setter that leaps
from one element to the next
in the spirit of play
the shape-shifter.

The quicksilver terrier
who burrows and darts
the riddler of vermin,

and last but not least
the wolf-hound
the great beast of war
who hunts after his own kin

our sharp-toothed conscience
the noble heart of allegiance.

XIV. the forest of things

Today we are children
lost in the forest of things
our hounds scattered
the lights of home far behind
the contours
the edges
the lines between air and mass
grow indistinct
they long to regain
their original ignorance
of their own shapes
the innocence of not being seen by us
they dream
of being discovered again
by someone else
animals
dogs
let them come
and recall
having found a mouse nest here
and rejoiced at the quick gulp of flesh
the forest of things is alive
it rearranges itself—
the dance of clawfeet and locks
at the edge of perception
a stir

against the backs of our hands
and subtle the grace
of keys losing themselves in the crowd
of book-spines slipping into
each other's spots
to hug the wrong pages
and strangle the bookmarks
the salad bowl
we had to bring to the party
that once
filled with almonds and beets
is lost irretrievably
turned
a blood-shot glass eye
in the shaggy forehead
of a mossy boulder
somewhere
terriers dig
noises come from above
and below
the trail of breadcrumbs
someone had left for us
rots

XV. your secrets

This is how you know where to keep your secrets:
an orchard persists in the heart
of the forest of things.
Its rows spaced even and wide
once well considered

its aging branches low enough
to reach
though bent to another's height
and loyal
and honest
in their work of bearing fruit.
You may read elsewhere
of apples that glow
to show the way. Of pale orbs,
smooth,
certain to catch the spare
autumnal sunlight
and restive
content in the trappings of grass.
A chorus.
A court
to every leaf that descends
unhurried like an abdicating monarch.
The orchard
is a student of gravity.
It has measured the surreptitious
contributions of worms
and sketched many times
rain's silent contortions
in the veins of its bark.
What needs here speak?
Words take their leave.
The tongue aches
for the sour hardness of apples.

canine ways

such simple canine ways of love we've learned

to see you walk into a room and be upright
assured of purpose as a compass needle drawn
delighted to its chosen north

to give the gift of nap—
a body so at rest it cannot help but lure another one
to bed

to heed the lesson of celestial dogs—
and be a playmate,
to cheer, be game—the greatest virtue of them all—
the will and wish to throw oneself into the other's call

airfield dreams

This is how a dream of the heroic begins:
with transport planes—two dashes in the sky,
a Morse-code M punched through the vellum
of air dense above the concrete
when they land, one, two, the rhythm so perfect
it trains the breath and stirs up a new hunger.

You watch the blur
of the propellers resolve into a slow churn, discern
the tread on tires and understand these are
workhorse machines flown by people
who can find the strip
in mud, and darkness, and whatever else
third-world calamity. That's when you tell yourself:
whatever faults we have,
we do purvey
a brand of well-orchestrated deliverance.

race day

we had called the ambulance
moments after the man collapsed
an event none of us really saw
lined at the rail to watch the start
his buzzed gray temples felt warm
as I lifted his head—but clammy
I could see sweat on his forehead
his pale lips
we asked his name
address
which horse he bet on
The Mongol, he said

The Mongol was the favorite
I worked the odds—
the men in this country die
ten years ahead of the women
most of heart attack or stroke
the man said nothing hurt
but then
his eyes—watery blue—lost focus
the lips went white   I felt his weight
collapse against my hips
behind me I could hear the trotters down the stretch
The Mongol boxed in
my pick Flying Dutchman surging
a gray ghost in his ragged rigging
of sweat
I patted the flabby cheek

The Mongol still has it, I said
the bell rang—
and the siren—
he muttered
I didn't have time to place the bet

each spring in moscow

wrens

three
four
    a flock
enter
the tussock of pampas grass
decorative in the middle
of a mown lawn

zig-zag
test mass
velocity
the way each stem accepts a body
and springs back when it lifts off
the plumes open and close
a mannerist
sentient fan

at last
all six find perch along
a single gleaming rod
that holds aloft
and inches above ground

they have arranged themselves
to their non-Euclidean satisfaction
seem content
then
gone
the grass and I alone again
without regret

crows, march

I spy:
a crow couple
besotted
considering their incipient nest

they catch sight of me
stare me down
from the height
of the birch
and their pugnacious
omnivorous love

each spring in Moscow

snow cowed
into an afterthought
dust spins up—
it is giddy
     airborne
          triumphant—
it feels like it's going places

settles for my shoes in the end
abrades the suede
unknits the socks
a small thwarted thing
turned to damage

soft targets

*On May 5, government forces disperse protests
against President Putin's fourth term.*

I cannot help it:
I picture damage
when in crowds
at the check-in line at the airport, say,
a metro station during rush hour
I project the direction of an imagined blast
shatter the nearest glass in my mind's eye
decompose the scene into carnage

this is also writing: power must
inscribe itself onto a body—

a reporter pulls up his t-shirt
in a cell-phone photo to show the red welt—
a strikethrough mark—left by a whip
wielded by someone dressed up as a Cossack

the singe of contact
is a Rubicon crossed
the broken ribs register on the BBC
the human rights report
one welcomes touch for the memory of it

last week a large horse gently
worked his whiskered lips on my cheek
we are all soft
soft targets

Russia: off-nominal

On November 28, 2017, Meteor, a Russian spacecraft carrying a payload of 22 satellites, lost contact with mission control three hours after launch. The working theory is that the navigation system had not been adjusted to the new launch site, causing the engines to fire too early, to correct what it perceived to be the wrong course.

now up there it hangs
on an inscrutable orbit
a gravity-bound fist
that will not unclench

the carrier launched with elation
an autotelic triumph rising out of the billows
of dust and exhaust like the Kremlin's cone
propelled by a parade's long-roiling banners—
a revolution re-staged

we watched the stages fall open
like offering hands—
except of course it was the simulacra
we saw, models of nominal flight—
only the myriad eyes of small satellites
blinked away glittering gusts of debris
to search the space
where more would flock

but the Meteor—with a stolen name like an alias
or a clairvoyant's warning—
was doomed when it looked for home.

flight patterns

Maidens' Field Park, Moscow, June

new parents drift along the paths
aimless as the cottonwood fluff that clogs
their stroller's wheels
a flock of pigeons
has occupied a bench
their droppings on its slatted back
a scrawled notation for a mad genius's oratorio

I sketch

a sick or wounded crow is on the ground
waiting to die in the shelter of hostas
it has made itself small
the shape of a human heart

a girl approaches opens with an excuse me
we converse
she maintains the crow is sick
tells me about the time she and a cousin
met a cat in this park and wanted to take it home
where there is one cat she points out
there's bound to be another
she is concerned about the crow
refuses to think its end
might be much nearer than a hypothetical cat
but approves of the sketch
we part

at the end of the alley
a memorial
three men in bronze
the long-range aviation pioneers
forever taking off to war
dwarf me
and the girl in her world
where cats ought to be taken home
and birds exist to be drawn

jet lag

awake
to the dim
obsidian mass of sky
black lacerations of trees
and a secretive rain
that tapped
a minute ago
in my dream
on a different
now so distant
window

CPSIA information can be obtained
at www.ICGtesting.com
Printed in the USA
BVHW042237201022
649968BV00001B/2